Everybody Just C@lm the F#ck Down

Also by Robert Chafe

Drama
Robert Chafe Two Plays: Butler's Marsh and Tempting Providence
Afterimage
Oil and Water
Under Wraps
The Colony of Unrequited Dreams
Between Breaths

Fiction
Two-Man Tent

Children's Fiction
Shiny and New

Everybody Just C@lm the F#ck Down
ROBERT CHAFE

Playwrights Canada Press
TORONTO

LIBRARY AND ARCHIVES CANADA CATALOGUING IN PUBLICATION
Title: Everybody just c@lm the f#ck down / Robert Chafe.
Other titles: Everybody just calm the fuck down
Names: Chafe, Robert, author.
Description: A play.
Identifiers: Canadiana (print) 20220221111 | Canadiana (ebook) 20220221197
| ISBN 9780369103475 (softcover) | ISBN 9780369103482 (PDF)
| ISBN 9780369103499 (HTML)
Classification: LCC PS8555.H2655 E94 2022 | DDC C812/.54—dc23

Playwrights Canada Press operates on land which is the ancestral home of the Anishinaabe Nations (Ojibwe / Chippewa, Odawa, Potawatomi, Algonquin, Saulteaux, Nipissing, and Mississauga), the Wendat, and the members of the Haudenosaunee Confederacy (Mohawk, Oneida, Onondaga, Cayuga, Seneca, and Tuscarora), as well as Metis and Inuit peoples. It always was and always will be Indigenous land.

We acknowledge the financial support of the Canada Council for the Arts, the Ontario Arts Council (OAC), Ontario Creates, and the Government of Canada for our publishing activities.

Canada Council Conseil des arts
for the Arts du Canada

ONTARIO ARTS COUNCIL
CONSEIL DES ARTS DE L'ONTARIO
an Ontario government agency
un organisme du gouvernement de l'Ontario

Canadä

ONTARIO | ONTARIO
CREATES | CRÉATIF

for Howard

Foreword

BY SARAH GARTON STANLEY

Grief and the unknowability of things. It never ends. Where does it start?

For Robert and me, it started following the death of a beloved colleague, amid the altitude and beauty of Banff, Alberta, where we sat across from one another, in what felt like a classroom, snow pouring down, and I heard a very early version of what was to become this beautiful play. I felt like I was at the school of life.

Sometimes theatrical writing is graced with an incisiveness . . . a crack in the fibre of "an everyday sense of life." It is writing that offers audiences a preview before there is enough common language to categorize the moment. I feel this way about Robert's *Everybody Just C@lm the F#ck Down*.

In this work, Robert has made a mini monster/masterpiece about the terrors of living and the even greater anxiety of dying. Caught between these two treacherous islands, the island of life and the island of death, stands an anti-hero called Robert Chafe, trying to piece it together. The truth of it is this: both the writer and the anti-hero never will. Those two islands just don't join. You can never ever really know. Ever.

So, instead, we ride. We buckle up tight, jump on the back of this crotch rocket, and meet at the bar later to drink deep and tell our own stories of that unexpected curve on that wide-open stretch of highway. The ride, the drink, and the story that followed . . . all antidotes to the terror of the encroaching dying of the light and the not knowing when that light will die. *Everybody Just C@lm the F#ck Down* is not for the faint of heart. But neither is living.

In 1974, Ernest Becker won the Pulitzer Prize for his book, *The Denial of Death*. In it he said, "To live fully is to live with an awareness of the rumble of terror that underlies everything."

Every day presents unexpected challenges, and most of us use stories to shore ourselves up for this inevitability, to empower ourselves in the face of it. Robert the character, and Robert the playwright, knows this only too well. Loss comes. It just does. Since we first showed this piece in St John's, Robert's brother passed away swiftly and with next to no warning. No one could have known. And so, in readying for publication Robert makes adjustments to the text and I make adjustments to these words.

We keep adjusting. We keep trying to make up for what we cannot know. We are always and forever one step behind.

Everybody Just C@lm the F#ck Down encourages us to make some peace with all the uncertainty. Impossible, really, which makes it a heartbreaking project for a character like our anti-hero Robert Chafe to attempt.

Director, dramaturg, and creator Sarah Garton Stanley is originally from Montreal, is a former associate artistic director of English Theatre at Canada's National Arts Centre, founding artistic director of SpiderWebShow, co-founder of FOLDA, and a former artistic director of Buddies in Bad Times Theatre. She has been the recipient of the Literary Managers and Dramaturgs of the Americas's Elliott Hayes Award, a Manitoba Theatre Award for best direction, and an Honorary Member Award from the Canadian Association for Theatre Research. She is finishing a Ph.D. in Cultural Studies at Queen's University and in 2020 she and her partner became co-stewards of the legendary Birchdale in Nova Scotia.

Everybody Just C@lm the F#ck Down was first produced by Artistic Fraud at the LSPU Hall in St. John's on July 31, 2021, with the following cast and creative team:

Writer and Performer: Robert Chafe
Director and Dramaturg: Sarah Garton Stanley
Additional Dramaturgy: Emma Tibaldo
Lighting Design: Leigh Ann Vardy
Sound and Video Design: Brian Kenny
Sound and Video Assistant: Julian Smith
Stage Manager: Crystal Laffoley
Technical Director: Sheldon Downey
Production Manager: Abra Whitney
Production Assistant: Robyn Vivian
Producer: Patrick Foran

Everybody Just C@lm the F#ck Down was written with the generous assistance of the Canada Council for the Arts and ArtsNL. The play was developed with the assistance of the 2018 Banff Playwrights Lab (a partnership between the Banff Centre for Arts and Creativity and the Canada Council for the Arts), as well as Playwrights' Workshop Montréal's 2019 Gros Morne Playwrights' Residency. The author and Artistic Fraud would also like to acknowledge the Corner Brook Arts and Culture Centre and its staff for a developmental technical residency in September 2019.

Notes

The author is inexorably evoked in the text of this play. The character is Robert: a Newfoundland playwright, a cisgendered queer white man of a certain age. It is the author's contention that these facts can't be separated from the spoken text without doing dramaturgical damage to the show. It's also the author's contention that any performer could, and should, embody the Robert that exists in this play and act as the temporary presentational vessel for this story. The author thinks that would be particularly interesting if that performer's body were in striking contrast to Robert's own: a different age, gender expression, race. The author thinks that explicit and intentional contradiction to the text detail would be very cool.

Stage directions are in *italics*. They are all intentional. Some may be spoken aloud.

A theatre.

People.

The stage is empty and black, except for a projection on the black back wall: footage of rain beating against a window.

There is nothing on the stage except for a small high table and a glass of water.

Formal. Staid. A lecture.

ROBERT enters: dress pants, dress shirt, jacket, and a cellphone in his hand. He walks centre, and with his phone he cues the house lights and video out and a spotlight up.

He stands in it a second, regarding the audience.

Hello.

I'm Robert Chafe.

I was born in St. John's and raised in the Goulds. Newfoundland. Canada.

I am forty-nine years of age, at least for the next couple of weeks.

And in September of 2008 I threw out my back.

Beat.

I was going to the gym, getting out of the car, and then deep in the small my back I felt this little—

He cues a sound—ping.

I was going to the gym because I had just been dumped after five-and-a-half months by this guy, and I was feeling suddenly very big and very old, and, as they say, the best revenge is a life lived well, so I was hitting the gym every day and eating nothing but dry turkey sandwiches in an effort to be effortlessly thin the next time I accidentally ran into him at the coffee shop he went to every morning between nine and ten.

I had just turned thirty-seven. And as I was getting out of the car that day, I was feeling good and energized and proud of my progress and then—

Ping.

And then . . . nothing, really. No pain right away, just a sense that something had . . . shifted.

I walked to the gym and got on the elliptical, all with this little ache blooming and steadily growing, so that by minute five of my workout I was so eclipsed by the ever-sharpening fire in my body I had to abandon everything and walk away in defeat, bent in half by it.

The pain continued unabated for weeks. I couldn't stand up straight.

I went to see a doctor. No real insight. Over-the-counter pain meds. Sure.

I was recommended two chiropractors: crack and crunch. No thanks.

My pain persisted.

With time, it began to feel consequential. Like I'd taken an irreversible turn in my life. Like my hard-living past might be catching up to me. I looked up diseases on the Internet. I worried about bone cancer.

And yet I didn't believe any of it. It all felt overly dramatic somehow. A distant story of what happens to other people. Something that could never, ever happen to me.

In month two, a friend recommended a different kind of chiro. No cracking, Robert. Muscle massage and gentle repositioning. She's great, Robert. I decided to give it a go.

Her office is very calm. Like . . . too calm. Like . . . intrusively serene. There's Buddhist iconography everywhere, a tiny water feature in the corner.

The receptionist presents me with an eight-page questionnaire, it being my first visit. Family history. My eating habits, embarrassing. Do I lie? Like she won't know it's a lie just by looking at me. Yes, processed foods. Yes, sugar. Yes yes yes. Memories of elliptical machines and dry turkey sandwiches seem so long ago. I was on the road to making a change in this body until this body broke and got in the way.

Have you suffered any physical or emotional trauma in the last year? No. Tick.

When the chiro finally takes me in, she sits me on a nice comfy chair overlooking the lake. It's raining outside, water beating against the window. There's an examination bed centre room, implements of her trade, things I'd never seen before and didn't recognize.

She's nice.
She looks too young to carry any amount of knowledge. I feel like I've seen her before, at a bar, on a dance floor, or—
Even if she's ten years younger than you, Robert, she's still old enough to be a specialist. That's how old you are now, Robert. Accept it, live it.

She starts going through the questionnaire. Digs into my preoccupation with diet soda, "unpacks" it. Tells me to drink lemon juice every morning to clear its toxins from my liver.

This is not a test, but I feel like I'm failing. This is a place where athletes come to hone their instruments. This is a place to prevent damage, not repair it. I find myself wondering if they might be wondering if I might be the heaviest person to have ever sat in this chair.

No physical or emotional trauma, she asks.

She's holistic. I get it now. The body as a manifestation of the mind. My cynicism is circling. I'm doing my very best to keep it at bay.

No, I say.

You sure? No trauma at all? No injuries? Falls? Broken bones?

Wait.
Yes.
Sorry.
Sorry.
I broke a rib.

You broke a rib?

Yeah. Late last winter. I was running across the parkway and . . .

I was leaving my boyfriend's place and I was running across the Parkway because the light had changed further down and the traffic was starting to flow towards me and so I was running, and when I hit the grass at the edge of the Parkway there was some black ice under the thin layer of snow, and I went down fully and the whole untended weight of me landed hard and my chest hit this block of old ice and I didn't know what had happened it happened so quick—I was running and then I was on the ground and I couldn't breathe and I was right by the side of the Parkway, cars zipping by, the sizzle and mist of their tires on the wet pavement and no one even stopped to see if I was okay.

I don't know how long I was lying there.

> *Pause.*

> I'd call that physical trauma, she says.
> And maybe even emotional trauma. Anything else?

No.

> No other emotional trauma?

Pfft. No.

> You sure?

Uh huh.

> No stress at work?

Nope.

> Spousal stress?

Definitely not.

Death in the family?

Pause.

Any deaths in the family?

Yes, I mean . . .
My grandmother.
She died in February.
I don't know why I forgot that.

Your grandmother died?

Yes.

Were you close?

Yes.

And . . .

And three weeks before that, my friend. I had a friend. Her name was Michelle. And she died. Suddenly.

Beat.

She was thirty-four.

And four months pregnant.

So . . .

Pause.

He looks at the audience, free suddenly from the memory.

And then . . . I burst into tears.

He cues a blackout and a video and music.

A song, old and romantic.

The rain against the window mutates into images of ROBERT
*hiking in the desert, splashing his feet in water, windswept on
beaches, skipping through fresh snow, being silly, living his best life.*

The ROBERT *in the video looks heavier physically but lighter
somehow: spiritually, emotionally.* ROBERT *knows this.*

*One final childhood picture, all smiles and innocence,
and then—*

The video cuts.

He has cut it short.

He looks at the blank back wall a moment, and then—

There are only a few episodes of television I remember from my
youth. Storylines where I remember, like, details, specific plot
points. The rest is just a big blur of feathered hair and mom jeans.

I remember an episode of the *Golden Girls*. Dorothy is sick. Tired
all the time. She goes to the doctor, but he dismisses her, tells
her she's fine. Can't find a thing wrong with her. But yet, she feels
sooooo bad.

She despairs. She gets depressed. Her symptoms persist. Her symptoms get worse. She starts to feel like she might be . . . crazy.

She finally searches out another doctor who tells her that she might have this newly identified condition called chronic fatigue syndrome. Dorothy eventually ends up confronting that first dismissive doctor in a restaurant:
"Dr. Budd. You probably don't remember me. I'm Dorothy, Dorothy Zbornak."

She tells him how afraid she was, how alone. Without a diagnosis.

Beat.

Now, why would a perfectly healthy seventeen-year-old kid from the Goulds, Newfoundland, hold on to that?

Why above all else would I remember that?

He cues a picture on the back wall—a hearty breakfast.

This is the breakfast Iris makes for me.

Iris was my dramaturg. A dramaturg is an early collaborator in the development of a play, a person who questions, provokes, motivates a playwright. And before she died a few years ago, Iris's process of dramaturgy involved a lot of shouting, chastising, cursing, smoking, and . . . cooking.

We are working at her place, and she has commanded me to show up hungry. It is January 2014 and I have just successfully defended my master's thesis, and we are, in part, celebrating. I take this picture before I eat and post it on Facebook with the following caption: "Iris Turcott made me a celebratory brunch. Call the ambulance now."

He cues an arrow on screen to point out each item as he speaks about it.

So, what you're looking at here are some hash browns with wieners in them, some eggs scrambled in bacon fat, some onion rings of course because what's breakfast without onion rings. And then for balance you've got some tomato slices, some bell pepper, a full half of a pineapple sliced, and of course a bowl of Halloween chocolate.

Iris loved to feed me, often against my will. When we'd eat together at a restaurant and the waiter would say, "Could I interest you in some dessert," Iris would say, "Nothing for me, but he'll have the cake!"

I suppose I encouraged this bad behaviour. I mean, I did eat the fucking cake. Every single time.

He cues the picture out.

An hour after eating this, I have heart palpitations. We are in Iris's local thrift store, looking for blue glass—she loved blue glass—and I start to feel dizzy and faint, and I am sweating a cold sweat and it feels like someone is gently laying their hand on me here. Right here, below my left armpit. It's a weird place for someone to lay their hand, so it's a weird feeling. I don't let Iris know what is going on. I mean I literally just posted a joke about calling an ambulance. So I don't say or do anything really. But I do think: when I get back home, I'm going to go see a doctor about this.

Home is St. John's. I am in Toronto. But I am heading to Saskatchewan.

I'm booked to do a reading at the University of Regina. Two days later, post bacon-fat eggs, and two hours before my reading, I am having dinner in an Earls with the theatre department head and a local playwright. I am eating a kale salad, and they are both talking to me, and I am kinda tuned out, preoccupied with what's going on in my chest, and then, surprising even myself, I look across the table at them and say: I'm sorry, but I think I'm having a heart attack.

They think I'm joking. I must be joking. A veeeery weird moment. So I shrug and apologize, and then they get that I'm not joking. They mobilize. They pay the bill, the department head cancels my reading. She drives me to the emergency department. I'm feeling bad. They flew me all the way to Regina and now my reading is cancelled. I only had a kale salad. I'm apologizing a lot.

It isn't until I'm in the emerg and talking to the triage nurse that I get to say it again: I think I'm having a heart attack.

Holy fuck. I think I'm having a heart attack.

I break in two. Crying, ug. Always with the crying. And in public. People are staring. And then I say: I'm really scared. I haven't said those words and really meant them since I was a little kid.

They listen.
They hook me up to a machine.
They take some blood.
They tell me I'm not having a heart attack and then they sit me in the waiting room. The theatre department head is kind. She sits with me. Twelve hours before she had never met me, and now here she is all but holding my hand and walking me towards midnight. I finally convince her to leave me, tell her that I will be fine. But once she's gone, this clutching despair circles. As each person in the waiting room is called away. I don't want to be alone. I'm in a hospital but I don't feel safe. I am still sweating that cold sweat, that invisible hand under my armpit, things in my body that I've never felt before, things my body knows are wrong. My cellphone is dying. Maybe I am too.

Two a.m. They admit me. They tell me that they are going to hold me for the night. More tests. A handsome young nurse comes in to insert an IV and I tell him about my phone. I'm tired and scared and I know I'm making it sound more serious than need be, but he goes and gets his own charging cord. He puts the IV in my arm while I watch his face. He's young, clean-shaven. The start of his shift. His hair is so dark, if this was the end of his shift his five o'clock shadow would give it away. When he's finished, he asks me if I felt the needle going in. I say no, even though I had. He tells me it's his first unsupervised IV insertion. He's very proud. I want to tell him about my thirty-four-year-old friend who went into the hospital and never came out. But the handsome young nurse is handsome, so I don't say anything.

In the middle of the night I wake up and my bed is wet. I think it's sweat. But when I look the sheets are pink. My IV has come loose and it's leaking saline and my blood all over the bed. My phone is charged and unplugged, the cord gone. I look at the time, do the calculation for home, three and a half hours ahead.
Early morning.
My father shirtless at the kitchen table eating cereal.
My mother in her chair by the window, tea going cold on the table. Thinking about me, where I am, and what I must be up to. Worrying. Always worrying, my mother.
I decide not to call.

The day-shift doctor comes in at nine with the results of the tests. She tells me that I'm . . . constipated.
Like, seriously.
Like, seriously so.
Like, that's what the x-ray showed up. For real. Shit. Who knew shit could show up on an x-ray?

Beyond that, she says . . . you're fine.

I'm fine.

What about the dizziness and sweating?

You're fine.
What about the hand under my armpit?
You're free to go.

They ask me if I have anyone to call to come get me. I say no. And so they call me a cab instead.

He cues a video: a POV shot of driving a rural prairie road in winter.

Regina looks different in the daylight. It's so flat and sandy, the antithesis of home. I'm trying to make conversation with the cab driver but he's having none of it. I've missed my flight back to Toronto. I extend my stay at the hotel for the night.

Alone, back in my room, and again I put off calling my mother. I plug my phone in even though it has 83% battery. I sit on the edge of my bed. I don't want to lie down. I'm hungry but I don't want to eat.

I'm afraid the housekeeping staff will find me in the morning. I'm afraid that no one will know what happened.

I'm afraid I'm going to die in Regina, in the humbling embrace of a three-star Travelodge.

ROBERT cues a blackout.

The video continues to play. Screenshots of his social media. Photos of him in Regina looking very sick. Photos of him in the hospital. A shot out the window of a plane, the sea covered in ice.

Status update: I've never been so happy to be home.

Snow gently falling on a St. John's park.

Memories, otherwise benign, are tinged now with something else. The past is trauma. The present provides no relief. The future is unknowable.

The video and song cut.

He has again cut them short abruptly. But this time he is looking over at the glass of water on the table.

There is now a slow drip . . . drip . . . drip from above. The drops land in the glass with light plops.

He watches it a moment.

And then:

My symptoms.

From that night in hospital in Regina and for the following three months I have a constant pain here in my lower right gut, and here in my upper left shoulder. I have that hand-under-my-armpit pressure. There's a general queasiness, pasty, I'm constantly covered in a thin film of sweat. I'm dizzy, but from deep inside. Not my ears, somewhere farther in. The room shifts with it, like I'm falling asleep and falling off my chair, but I'm not moving. And sometimes, when it's really bad, the light is crowded out, darkness at the periphery of my eye line pushes itself centre, like I'm passing out, but I'm wide awake and watching it happen.

After the third month the pain in my gut and chest goes away, as does the hand under my armpit. The dizziness stays, intensifies, and brings a tinnitus. My ears are ringing all the time. My head swells up, feels like it's full of cotton. Like the worst cold of my life. Headaches, I can't breathe through my nose. This settles in and stays, unabated . . . for two years.

And then the shooting pains in my head. Unpredictable. A bolt of lightning across my scalp and then deeper in that makes my eyes cross for a second. The tingling in my fingers. That week the entire side of my face went numb. I used to go to the hospital because I was having a heart attack, now I go because I'm having a stroke.

It's all hard to describe, and I've had lots of practise. My family doctor an ENT a neurologist a rheumatologist a cardiologist a naturopath an allergist a physio a chiropractor my dentist. I've had CT scans MRIs colonoscopies nasal scopes stress tests blood work blood work and more blood work, you're fine. They all say it, "You're fine, Robert."

Everyone except for the neurologist.

He says: "Well, you don't have the debilitating neurological condition that you are here, after a seven-and-a-half-month wait, to terrifyyyyyingly get tested for, but . . . have you ever thought about losing some weight?"

A pause.

ROBERT *angrily reaches into his pocket and pulls out a clown nose.*

He puts it on and cues a lighting shift. A spotlight.

He stares at the audience blankly for a long time.

A long time.

Then:

Is there a doctor in the house?

He takes the nose off quickly.

He cues the lights to restore.

Iris would always say to me, "You're not funny, stop trying to be funny." It usually would be me trying to add some poorly placed levity in a show.
Stop it, Robert, you're not funny. Just tell the goddamn story.

He looks at the nose, for a second, and then puts it back in his pocket.

Pause.

I ask my nice family doctor about chronic fatigue syndrome. Her look alone tells me I'm fishing. I've been seeing her for a little over fifteen years, and she tells me to feel free to ask her anything. So . . . I go online and type my symptoms into Google, I know, I know I'm not supposed to do it. I save what I find on my phone and bring it back to her. She sits in her chair and I lob conditions across the room at her like an oral final exam. Lyme disease, you've been tested twice. Celiac disease, you've been tested twice. Thyroid, tested three times, your levels are normal. Diabetes, blood sugar is fine. The list gets thin—each time the list gets thin with no answer in sight, and I want to throw my fucking phone at the wall, and each time the last thing on the list is what I regard to be the least likely, and she agrees, she says to me, I've known you for a long time, Robert, the profile just doesn't fit, you just don't seem like a . . . an anxious person.

My doctor tells me that she has sleepless nights wondering about what's going on with me.
And I'm like: "Come on, you have over two thousand patients." And she says: "Yes, Robert, but I see you a lot." She tells me that she's driven by the mystery, which is nice, because I am too. I just want

an answer. It's been over six years now. When I had the CT scan I was actually hoping it would show something.

I cried when it didn't.

He smiles.

He shouldn't have thought that. And he knows it.

What he doesn't know is that in six months' time his older brother Howard will have a CT scan that actually does show something. Glioblastoma. Aggressive brain cancer.

But ROBERT doesn't know that yet. On this night, in this theatre, ROBERT is oblivious to what is to come.

Tennessee Williams choked to death on the cap of a bottle of eye-drops. It's surmised that his gag reflex was hindered by his constant use of alcohol and prescribed drugs. It was said he was taking a whole host of shit in hopes of stemming the tide of a bunch of minor or imagined ailments. He was so terrified of getting sick, he got sick and died.

Am I Tennessee Williams?

Or am I Dorothy Zbornak?

Am I a lonely hunter in the search for an objective truth that currently only I know exists?
Or am I the jaded storyteller, falling victim to my own catastrophic imagination?
Is the problem in my body? Or in my mind?
Am I sick? Am I really really sick?
Or am I just . . . ?

He cues a video: his head, various shots and angles, time-lapsed, jolting, erratic.

ROBERT *walks into a new light centre stage.*

Occasional flickers of light and sound, like little zapping shocks.

Throughout the following the water glass finally fills and begins to slowly spill over the table and onto the stage.

I wake up with shooting pains in my head. They're sharp and run from my eyes to the back of my scalp, not connected to my heart-beat, isolated and random. And with every one I can feel my sense of balance shift and wobble, like if I was standing up I'd totally be falling down. I think I might be having a stroke, but then I think no, no, this has happened before and you've gone to the hospital and there was nothing wrong. And then I think, but maybe they missed something, and then I think they gave you a fucking CAT scan, Robert—

Zap.

—chill out and go back to sleep. And I try. But I can't. I want to know what time it is, and I want to check, but my cellphone is plugged in on the other side of the room. And then I think I really should remember to get an extension cord that reaches behind the bed so that I can plug in my phone a little closer to me or plug in my laptop in case I wake up with a good idea instead of waking up with shooting pains. And then I'm thinking about my computer and how much I have on it and the last time I might have backed it up and that I should really back it up and that I really should have brought it upstairs with me because what if there was a break-in—

Zap.

—and they took it, I mean my life is on that computer, unfinished work, stuff I'm excited about, proud of, stuff I'm not so proud of, stuff that's private, very very private—

Zap.

—and then I'm more stressed about someone accessing my computer than I am about them stealing it and then I remember that it has a security lock. And then I'm thinking about screen savers and how they have evolved, how they used to be all abstract and trippy and how now all the screen savers are nature pictures, polar bears and penguins getting ready to jump and leopards in tall grass, and lush green valleys and how IT'S ALL A LIE—

Zap.

—and that screen savers really should be pictures of the factories in China and landfills filled with plastic wrap and scrap electronics. And then I'm thinking that screen savers are like everything else we surround ourselves with—they're just a DESPERATE ATTEMPT to forget what we are and what we've done to the world, and that's what TV is like too.

And art is like that a lot of the time.

Theatre, for sure.

I've made theatre like that.

For the first time, something he hasn't cued: the slowly growing drone of a voice dominated by static, ominous in its incomprehensibility.

Suddenly warm, ROBERT begins to take off his jacket.

And I'm thinking about that, and TV, bad TV, and sports, professional sports, and then I'm thinking about professional sports and
how it's really only a sanitized way of feeding our deep-seated
need to be combative and pack-driven without actually shedding
blood. And then I'm thinking that's not all sports, surely, but maybe
just team sports, because stuff like synchro or the hammer throw
doesn't really hold the same thrill so obviously people watch those
for pure reasons, an appreciation of the skill and athleticism, and
then I'm thinking that no, fuck, that no—

Zap.

He throws his jacket.

—people don't watch those sports at all unless there's a flag on the
person's shoulders and a medal count, so it's all the same thing
then, right? And then I'm thinking about Chomsky's comments
about professional sports being a grand distraction purposely
endorsed—IF NOT STAGED—by the powers that be to keep us occu-
pied while really consequential and truly catastrophic shit goes
down. And then I think I really should learn that quote so I can
whip it out at parties and in arguments, and then I think I should
look it up and that I really should have brought my computer
upstairs, and then I think I hear noise downstairs.

Sound out.
Stillness.
Silence.

And I stop breathing so I can listen.

Silence.

And I listen.

Silence.

And I listen.

Shhhh.

And then I start thinking about how loud or quiet an intruder could would should be for me to be able to hear them all the way up here in my bedroom, and then I have to breathe again, like I HAVE to breathe again, and so work on convincing myself that it was nothing.

It was really nothing.

It was probably nothing.

Just the house settling.

Even though it's really old and should have settled by now.

And then I'm thinking that safety and serenity are like a rickety house, a house too old, over-stressed, dangerous possibility of collapse, when the wind blows hard, or when it rains heavy, but most days it can manage to stand, it can keep it together just fine, this rickety old house of peace and calm. I can keep it standing just fine as long as I breathe, and so I do, I breathe, I breathe, and as I lie there breathing, five, four, three, two, and out through the nose, as I lie there breathing this old house of sanity is standing just fine.

Just fine.

Just. Fine.

And then I think I smell smoke.

Electronic drumbeat, furious, punching.

Video flashes: Smoke. X-rays. Skulls.

Escalating and disorienting.

Stop.

Voices repeating, samples from movies: calm the fuck down, calm the fuck down.

Stop.

But it won't stop.

One final scream: everybody just calm the fuck down!

Video snaps, light shifts.

Some guy messages me on Grindr:

Ping.

He says: "Nice profile picture, but aren't trolls supposed to be under bridges?"

And I reply: "Ah the bravery of headless men." 'Cause his profile picture was a faceless torso, of course it was, Grindr. And he says: "It was just a little joke, why are you getting so upset?" And I block him.

GO FUCK YOURSELF!

And then an hour later I realize my profile pic was taken under a bridge. Like, you can actually see the bridge in the background, sooooo . . . I don't know, I probably just read it wrong, right? Read it with the wrong emphasis, like I read it as, "Hey, aren't trolls supposed to be UNDER BRIDGES," when what he really meant was,

"Hey, aren't TROLLS supposed to be under bridges." As in, you are under a bridge but you're definitely not a troll, as in you are cute, as in he probably wasn't a dick, you guys, he was probably just being sweet and awkward and nerdy and he was probably the man of my dreams.

No. Something else.

I have this great new dentist. Kind, painless, PAINLESS! Utterly painless. I mean, my god, he just pulled this molar and . . . I mean I've had molars pulled before, several molars, eight years ago, Jesus, seveeeeral pulled because I was an artist and I had no dental insurance and no money so I didn't go to the dentist for twelve years and so my molars were rotting out and ANYWAY, my new dentist, he's great because that old dentist he pulled half of them, definitely not painless, and he tried to save the other half with these VERY expensive fillings and then just last month another one cracked mid-chew so my new sweet dentist, he had to pull it, and he's great, but now there is a gaping hole a bit too forward in my mouth and my tongue gets sucked into my cheek and I bite it when I chew sometimes or when I talk too much. I bite it fully, crunch, squelch, like an uncooked steak and whatever I'm eating tastes like blood and it bleeds and bleeds for hours and I have to bite down on medical gauze until it stops and my tongue swells and I can't eat anything but soup and pudding for a week until the swelling goes down but then inevitably I just bite it again and—!

No. Something else.

I have this fun thing where sometimes I designate times in my life by food trends. Like, that didn't happen when I was twenty-two, that happened during the hummus years. The jalapeno popper years, the sun-dried tomato years. The bread bowl years. I put on a lot of weight during the bread bowl years. And currently we are in the aaaage . . . of the cauliflower wing. And the Instant Pot, which I know isn't a food, but it's just so damn versatile.

Crumpled jacket on the floor like a body.

Versatile?! I once hit three separate fast-food chains in one single meal. I once got asked by the management of an all-you-can-eat Chinese buffet to "leave some chicken balls for the other people" when my great-grandfather passed away and the headline in the *Evening Telegram* read: "Newfoundland's Fattest Man Dies"!

You're not funny, Robert.

I was walking on this trail, and I passed this scruffy-looking guy, and he was carrying a bag of recycling, a piece of salvaged cardboard, and a blue highlighter. And he says, "Excuse me, quick question, are you a good person?" And I say, "Why?" And he says, "I'm doing a survey." And without a second thought I say, "Yes, I'm a good person." And he makes a note with his blue highlighter on his piece of cardboard and turns and keeps walking. And I turn and keep walking. But for some reason I can't shake it, you know, so I turn and yell down the trail to him, "I mean, I think so! I try to be!" And he shrugs, as if to say: sorry, your answer has already been recorded. And I turn and keep walking, but I can't stop thinking about it, am I a good person?

Am I a good person?

It was just a piece of cardboard and a fucking highlighter, Robert!

Something else.

It's become a routine part of my day to smile at myself.

In bathroom mirrors. Elevator mirrors. Rear-view mirrors.

To make sure my face is not lopsided.

To make sure I'm not having a stroke.

Ping.

Ping ping ping.

Ping.

Ping ping ping ping ping ping ping ping ping ping ping ping—

The first time I was ever on a plane, I was sixteen years old and I saved up for two whole years and paid my own way on a student trip to Italy and Greece. The company offering the trip specialized in affordable overseas vacays for kids: crappy hotels, chartered flights at weird times and circuitous routes, St. John's to Halifax to Boston to New York to Athens to Rome, thirty-two hours of flying, my first time ever on a plane, and I truly couldn't fathom how anyone could be afraid of such a thing. We hit an air pocket over Boston Harbour and dropped a couple of hundred feet, the water racing up towards us. It was like a roller coaster. I'd never been on one of those either. We were going from Rome to Naples to Athens and through the Greek islands by plane, bus, and boat. My itinerary was all written down on a piece of paper and stuck to the family fridge, and I told my mother I would call when I could. These were the Caesar salad and wine cooler years, well before the Internet and cellphones, and by the time I got an appointment at the international calling centre, she had been crying for two days. She thought I was dead because there had been a train crash.

In northern China.

No.

Something else.

Ignore those noises. An ominous drone, voices. Ignore them.

Speak calmly.

Put your hands in water.

Pick up or touch items near you.

Breathe deeply.

Savour food or drink.

Take a short walk.

Hold a piece of ice.

Savour a scent.

Move your body.

Listen to your surroundings.

Feel your body.

Try counting, five, four, three—

> *Not working. Something else.*

> Oh my god, you have lost so much weight.

Yeah.

> Like a ton of weight.

Yeah.

> Like a ton!

Yes.

You look great.

Oh, uh thanks.

Really. Great.

Thank you.

Not to say that you were ugly before.

Okay.

How are you?

Well I—

I mean, are you okay? Are you like . . . sick?

The weight loss was intentional.

Oh, so you don't have cancer or anything.

Jesus, no.

I mean . . . I don't think so.

No.

Don't think.

Don't think at all.

Catastrophe.

Waiting to happen. Dangling by a thread.

Even the weather is violent.

Trump.

There's no going back.

I'm not political! I hate confrontation. I mean, I can't even talk to conservatives because we disagree on everything, and I frustrate liberals because they demand action. So . . . so I just sit in the middle. Hoping for the best. And feeling like the worst, feeling like a quivering fucking invertebrate and wishing that I could just be—

Stop.

Most of the men in my family are on heart medication by the age of fifty. My grandmother raised twelve kids on a fisherman's income. When my great-grandfather passed away, the headline in the *Evening Telegram* read—

Something else.

May 25 and it's snowing outside, so of course global warming is a hoax, and suddenly a D in grade-ten science makes him an authority, and I'm nothing but a "stupid libtard" and I know I shouldn't even read the comments section and I definitely shouldn't waste my time responding to this fucking guy but—

Stop.

This business of getting on with it, this business of living, I am practising gratitude, practising gratitude, practising gratitude because it is true what they say—

Mom.

My mother says, "It's not funny." When we tease her for being so nervous all the time.
"You don't know what it's like, my son."

Something else.

Buddy is looking at me and my shopping cart because I have nothing in it but a six-pack of Coke Zero and a box of Pirate cookies, but he's the one not wearing his mask and having a root at his nose, and—

No.

I'm walking in the Arctic tundra, my lungs hurt when I breathe, there's no one else around, no signs of life at all, and I think I might be all alone on the planet, and then I see polar bear shit, with a chewed-up diaper in it.

Stop.

I've got something in my eye. And I can't see what it is. And that story doing the rounds on Facebook about that woman who had three tiny bees living inside hers, and they were surviving by drinking her tears.

Stop it. Breathe.

Am I dying? Or am I just afraid? Or am I just afraid of dying? Or am I just afraid because I'm dying? Or am I just dying because I'm afraid? Why would I be afraid? There's nothing to be afraid of. Except for dying. Am I dying?

No.

Do you know what happens when I shut up, 'cause I don't.

No!

Sometimes I watch videos of guys finding out they're going to be a dad. Or videos of babies laughing. It's nice to see people . . . surprised, by joy. Joy, it can feel so . . . so hard won, it . . .
It's nice to remember, sometimes it's nice to remember that it can just sneak up on you.
Unbidden. And I guess remembering that, meditating on that, that's what you call . . . hope.

Yes.

Breathe.

Okay.

A baby sitting in garbage. The baby is still smiling.

Breathe.

Take your time.

Everything can wait.

Hold your breath.

Listen. Quiet.

Okay.

Okay. Now breathe.

In her final years, Michelle was really nervous about flying. Like she almost lost a job because she was so suddenly terrified of flying. And she developed this latex allergy and she couldn't set foot in the door of a restaurant without calling over the hostess and making her pinky swear there was no latex in the kitchen and . . .

And she was only thirty-four, but she started asking friends to take her to the drugstore to use the blood pressure machine because she was just convinced that . . .

Breathe. It's okay.

The last picture taken of us was at a party on Old Christmas Day. She had this little cold over the holidays but then she got better and so she was at this party, and we were standing in a hallway and in the picture we are smiling. And she is in profile, her little baby bump, which is so fitting because that's what we were talking about. How excited she was to be a mom, but how terrified she was about giving birth. Very wary of the physiology.

Breathe.

And then a few weeks later, January 18, I had just joined the gym, first time in my life. Honey. New Year's resolution and living my best life, and so I was oblivious that morning—twenty-five minutes on the elliptical, ten on the rowing machine, twenty-five minutes on the treadmill, pecs, biceps, triceps, core planks—and I had my phone turned off, and when I turned it back on it just . . . it lit up.

Ping.

Ping ping ping.

Ping.

Ping ping ping ping ping ping ping ping ping ping ping ping.

Myocarditis.

It's an inflammation of the heart muscle caused by a viral infection. She had that little cold over Christmas. And then she got better. And then one night her heart started racing and they couldn't make it stop and then she died.

It's okay.

Breathe.

None of us saw it coming.

But . . . I don't know. Maybe she did?

Maybe she saw it coming. But she didn't know what it was.

Or how to stop it.

Something else.

Something else.

Remember that game? That old board game?

You'd get to play the doctor. The patient and his charley horse, writer's cramp. Butterflies in his stomach. You'd get to pluck out his broken heart, but if you touched the edge you'd get a zap.

The patient wore a red clown's nose.

No.

Okay.

Okay.

If you want to know what it's like, it's like . . .

It's like you're on a plane and . . . the seat-belt light is busted and won't turn off, but you know, somehow, you just know, that you've reached your cruising altitude. And you don't even know how long the flight is. Or how quickly you'll descend. Turns out there's not even a guaranteed meal on this flight, and your in-seat TV only plays the one movie—it's a documentary about success and happiness and you're not in it. And there's turbulence, lots of turbulence, and the flight attendants don't serve drinks anymore, they just stand in the aisle and demonstrate how to put on your life jacket. And suddenly you want nothing more than to be on the ground again. Which is totally weird and new because you always always always just wanted to go—

    Zap.

It's like you're going for a picnic and you're totally fine to eat whatever but a bit more picky about where you sit, but you're one of those extroverted introverts that people think will speak their mind but you won't because it will rock the boat and you're already seasick and so you let your friends pick where you're going to stretch out, a rough patch of grass with a nice view of the sea and all your friends are all sighing with relaxation because what could possibly be better except all you can see is that long-legged spider trying to make its way towards the cheese plate and you're not even thinking about the food anymore because you're peeling back the sod and pushing aside the rocks to see all the spiders and worms and earwigs and ants and eggs and maggots and the swirling wriggling biomass all over the food and all over your friends and in their mouths and just waiting to crawl up and over and inside you like an overturned grave just waiting to—!

    Zap.

It's like you're driving and there's no one on the highway and you're heading over the Holyrood barrens and the sky is cloudless and the moon is out and the radio is cutting in and out and the man on it is telling you that over a million species are at risk of extinction in our lifetime.

And then there are lights in your mirrors, in your eyes, and suddenly some guy flies past you like you're standing still, and his tires kick up salt and grit, and through the dirty sweep of your wipers you can't see his licence plate, but you can see the baby on board sign in his back window.

And then later, sure enough, later, you see his tail lights in the ditch and his car sitting on its head, and the horn is blaring, and you pull over and walk down to it and the windshield is broken and he's not inside, and you see his one bare foot shining in the headlights out there in the tall dead grass of the ditch, and you go to him. And you bend down to him. And your hands are on his body, holding parts of him in, hot red gushing through your fingers, his pupils dilated, tears washing tracks down his temples through the dirt and the blood. He's looking at you, the last of him in his eyes, just about to drain out his gut with the rest, but the last of him is still there in those big black pupils looking at you, looking to you, for you to offer some grace, some comfort. A baby's shoe in the ditch next to his head. And you lean in and you say . . . you say:

You were going too fast.

No.

I feel bad for my family doctor. You know?

Yesssss.

Like sometimes I feel really bad for her because I like her. She's kind, and before all this she just had to deal with the occasional flu from me and absentee notes and questionable benign growths and STDs and stuff.

STD scares.
I don't really . . .
I was cleared. Clean as a whistle.

I mean, who hasn't had a—

Zap.

I'm going through a drive-through and I want fried chicken but
I'm feeling gross so I decide to get a salad and then the kid behind
the window asks me how my day is going and I lie and say fine and
then he asks me if I'm working today and I tell the truth and say no,
and then he asks me if I'm retired and I say, "No, c'mon, I'm far too
young to be retired," and he says . . . "Really?"

Zap.

There are people who can only live in this world if they know they
have the power to change it.

There are people who can only live in this world if they know that
it's all totally beyond their control.

I walked past a Best Western Hotel and its LED sign was saying, "It
takes both sides to build a bridge." And all I could think was . . . who
hurt you, Best Western, who hurt you?

Zap.

No.

Zap.

Stop.

Zap.

Iris would tell me to stick to the story. She would—I think she would, wouldn't she? She would, I think. I don't know, I DON'T KNOW, how could I, she died too! Very inopportune time to up and die on me, Iris. All of this would have been a lot funnier if you had just thought I was funny.

Zap.

Stick to the goddamn—

Zap.

The story, okay, the story, all of the doctors and the tests, the order of the tests, the details of the tests, the neurologist—"You need to lose some weight" (thanks)—the allergist—"You're allergic to dust mites" (who isn't?)—the ENT with the nasal scope—"You're fine, sir, no obstructions," but I can't breathe through my nose—

Zap.

You're fine! The naturopath who did a very expensive blood test only to tell me that I had a "mild sensitivity to pecans" (uh oh), "and to chocolate" (fuck my life, is that what's doing this?). "It's very mild, sir." Don't tell me that's what's doing this, don't tell me it's chocolate, and she's like, "It's very mild, sir. You'd have to consume huuuuge quantities," and I'm like . . . "Define huge."

Zap.

The story, yes, my mother, Mom, Mommy, Mom, five kids, five kids and on her last one, the biggest one, after she was done and my baby brother, he was finally fully out, she was still in this crazy immense pain, and they were all like what is this twins, suddenly? And so they checked her out and they confirmed that she wasn't having twins but she was . . . passing a KIDNEY STONE!

At the same time.

As she was giving birth.

To a baby.

Through her vagina.

My mother is fucking fierce!

My mother was a fucking badass! Left home, sixteen years old, the town of Quirpon at the tippy top of the island of Newfoundland, took the coastal boat to the big city of St. John's by herself. 1957! Sixteen years old!

She had a beehive hairdo and wore long silk gloves and was flirty and fun and the life of the party.

My mother lived on that delicate line of danger and death and beauty and life and she loved it! She fucking loved it! She loved life and embraced the danger of it and was never afraid of it. She was never ever—

ZAAAAAP.

Don't cry.

Smile.

Don't cry.

Remember that song?

Yes, that song.

Old and romantic. You used to think about Michelle when you heard it. Even though she was only thirty-four and you were never romantic. But something about it made you think of her, find her again, even years after she died. She'd be clear and crystal in your memory just like that song. But now it sounds broken. That song. Like a radio station that's a few numbers off on the dial. Fractured, persistently pushing against static and decay.

Don't cry.

Don't you fucking cry.

Zap.

—or am just afraid because I'm dying, or am I just dying because I'm afraid. Why would I be afraid? There's nothing to be afraid of, except for dying. Am I dying, or am I just afraid, or am I just afraid of dying, or am I just afraid because I'm dying, or am I just dying because I'm afraid. Why would I be afraid, there's nothing to be afraid of, except for dying. Am I dying, or am I just afraid, or am I just afraid of dying, or am I just afraid because I'm dying, or am I just dying because I'm afraid. Why would I be afraid, there's nothing to be afraid of, except for—

There's nothing to be afraid of. Except for everything.

That TV show with the drag queens and they're talking about climate change and from their mouths it all sounds as harmless as you want it to be, but you know that it's not. Like everything else, it is not. You've seen the satellite images, the hurricanes swirling in red and orange and yellow and red, dizzying and terrifying and faster and faster.

There's nothing to be afraid of except for—

The thunderbolts across my scalp and the tingling in my fingers and that time the side of my face went numb and the Australian bush fires and families escaping into the sea. And a pain here and here and that hand under the armpit and just go back to sleep and that immigrant family who lost all of their kids in that house fire and the nice people who raised money for them and the other people who bitched about it and that ringing in my ears and just ringing and ringing and you've been tested three times, Robert, and people pissed about phone Amber Alerts for missing kids and wash your hands and wear your mask and you CAN'T MAKE ME and the Nazis are back! And DONALD FUCKING . . . and I'm not racist and QAnon and white pride and straight pride and Proud Boys and men's rights and you can't even look at a woman anymore and lock her up and build that wall and babies in cages and babies washing up dead on the beach and I just don't get why you're soooooooo fucking sensitive!

I keep biting my tongue.
I keep biting my tongue.
Everything tastes like blood.

Stop.

Breathe.

Close your eyes.

Don't.

Don't listen to that. An animal, a riot. It doesn't matter. It's outside. It's outside of these walls.

These little walls.

Breathe.

Breathe.

Just—

Breathe deeply.

Try.

Yes.

Take a short walk.

Can't move.

Pick up or touch items near you.

Move your body.

Can't.

Listen to your surroundings.

Try.

Feel your body.

Try counting.

Five.

Yes.

Four.

Three.

Two.

One.

He opens his eyes.

Light has transitioned to something wide and open, unlike anything we've seen. Exposed.

It is perfectly quiet.

He bursts into uncomfortable laughter. Relief.

He stands looking at us, laughing and trying to catch his breath.

After a moment, he walks to the glass of water. Picks it up for the first time, sips it.

Savour food or drink.

He drinks some more water. He spills it on his chin and shirt. Laughs at himself.

First day with the new mouth.

He wipes his mouth, flicks the excess off his hand.

He shows his hand to us. It's shaking. Badly.

He lowers his hand. A weak smile.

A long silence.

I really want to be able to . . . um . . .

Pause.

*He makes a decision. Through the following, he removes his
lapel mic.*

This is the part of the story where I tell you what the problem is.
The diagnosis.

Something not that serious. Or maybe in an unexpected twist,
something actually very serious and you've suddenly stumbled into
a real bummer of a story about . . .

Beat.

But you haven't.

And it's not.

And there really is no diagnosis. No answer.

And I still don't know if I'm Tennessee or Dorothy.

And I've done what I can, I think, all that I can. My neurologist told
me to lose some weight. Tried that, it didn't work.

Beat.

And I still have shooting head pains. And I still wake up in the
middle of the night and . . .

Beat.

It's fine.

Seriously. It's fine.

I mean, it's not fine, but it's fine, you know, strangely fine, like it shouldn't be fine but it is. Fine.

Like, you get a shooting pain in your head one day and it's . . . veeery alarming, and then you get a shooting pain in your head every day for five years, and it's . . . fine.

Shrug.

And I am grateful.

I mean, I should be grateful.

I am practising gratitude and I should be relieved, unquestionably, and I am. I mean, I do know how lucky I am, don't get me wrong. I know how lucky I am because I have friends with very real chronic illnesses, very real undebatable conditions, confirmed and named. I have friends who have . . .

Glioblastoma. His brother Howard will be completely non-symptomatic. And then out of nowhere, they'll give him twelve months to live. He'll only get two.

But ROBERT *doesn't know that.*

ROBERT *doesn't know that yet.*

When Iris got cancer she was very . . . cavalier about it all. Like she knew she was actually dying and she was very matter-of-fact about it. She gave out gifts, bequeathed things. She had notes and work plans for projects we were working on together. It's like stop, whatever, you're dying, you know, but she was all . . .

And even at her memorial service, they had it in a theatre, and the sign in the lobby said, "This Way Assholes." Because she used to swear like a sailor, you know? And everyone knew this about

her. She used to swear like a sailor, a drunk sailor, like a drunk
sailor who just stubbed their toe. And she smoked like a fucking
kiln, gave people horrible horrible nicknames. She used to call me
arse-flapper.

Pause.

And I mean you kinda wish for yourself to be like that. You know?
Just like . . . fuck it, you know? I mean, I know Iris wasn't totally
without . . . but she was, you know, she . . . I need to sit down.

My hips are hurting. I need a . . .

He suddenly leaves the stage.

After a moment . . .

*He returns with a chair from the wings and through the fol-
lowing he places it and sits.*

My hips are not good. When I threw out my back that time, at
the gym and the ex-boyfriend and the chiropractor and the . . . all
those years ago, they couldn't figure out what was wrong with me,
of course they couldn't, and so they sent me for x-rays and they
figured out that it wasn't my back at all, it was my hips. My back
was just compensating, it was actually my hips. Chronic and severe
arthritis. Hips of a seventy-year-old my nice family doctor said, no
offence to any seventy-year-olds. And she said, my doctor said, that
it might just be the way I'm naturally built, or I could end up need-
ing double replacement surgery.

He toasts with his water.

Pause. Then . . .

I really do want to be honest here, so . . .

In the spirit of that . . . a few notes and revisions.

Beat.

I didn't actually see polar bear shit with a diaper in it. That was from a post by a much more interesting friend on Facebook. I've never even been to the Arctic. I should probably get on that.

And I also didn't see a man die in a Holyrood ditch. That was just a . . . When a guy blew past me on the highway with a baby on board sign in his back window. One of those little mental movies, you know?

And I probably shouldn't be cracking jokes about STDs. It's just stigmatizing, and unnecessary.

And I definitely shouldn't be talking about how I'm not a political person, because it's not true. I am, of course I am, how could I not be, how could anyone.

Beat.

And . . . and I don't know for sure that my mother was ever without fear. But I guess that's my great wish for her.

Beat.

And believe me, I would love to end all this on a good note. I would love to show you a sweet video of babies laughing. Or something, but . . .

Pause.

Awkward.

He looks at the ceiling.

He looks through the ceiling.

A small smile.

Okay.

The story.

Beat.

Okay.

So . . . once upon a time . . . I would never be caught dead home alone on a Friday night. Truly. And these were the Mr. Noodle years, the age of no-name tuna. But nevertheless I'd happily drop fifty bucks at the club. Alone but determined. And in head-to-toe boy sequins—seriously, there are pictures, I wasn't shy. And I used to dye my hair jet black, and perhaps more notably I had hair to dye. And I used to smoke two packs a day and drank Manhattans by the pint with extended pinky and triple maraschino. And I always over-tipped the boys behind the bar so they wouldn't skimp on the pour and no one ever gave me shit for having martinis on the dance floor because, honey, she never spilled a drop let alone dropped a glass, and three drinks in and I'd flirt with the fucking Pope and I never had much of an ass but what I had I could shimmy and shake and that dance floor was beat into submission, and I would twirl, motherfucking twirl, as close to that damn speaker as possible because you're not hearing the music unless you're feeling it behind the eyes, "Ray of Light" and "Born Slippy" and "Big Time Sensuality," and that dance floor might be crowded but there's always room for a neighbourly grind, and the music is mine all mine and the room is thumping and my heart my heart my heart and Björk is just howling—

He sings:

I don't knooooooow my futurrrre after this weekeeeennnd . . . annnd
I don't want to!

Pause.

And I'd surprise myself on the regular. Sing in public without
immediately regretting it.

And I habitually wished my time away. Because somehow I had no
idea it was finite.

And there was nothing to be afraid of. Or at least that was a lot
easier to believe.

And gratitude was harder to summon. But much less necessary.

And people hardly ever died, but when they did it at least followed
some natural order.

And when they did you grieved, yes, but you didn't dwell, you didn't
sink into . . . dread, because you knew, you KNOW, that a person's
life deserves to be so much more than . . .

Pause.

And there was no holding on.
There was no holding on to anything. Because you can't hold on
when you're letting go.

Beat.

Some terrifying night in a Regina hospital.

The person you might have been.

The person you were before.

That carefree black-haired boy twirling on the dance floor.

Pause.

He thinks.

Shakes his head.

He raises the glass of water, looks at, then defiantly he chugs most of it, and tips the rest over his head.

Dripping, he tosses the glass over his shoulder and it bounces away.

He reaches into his pocket and pulls out the clown nose. He displays it.

I . . . fully admit . . . that part of me started all of this in the hopes that one of you might come up to me and say I know exactly what is going on with your body, it's called this, and this is how you fix it.

Or maybe at least one of you might say, hey you've got it all wrong. There is nothing to be afraid of. And then give me a really good reason why that's true.

He looks at us a moment.

No takers.

He slowly puts the nose on.

A deep breath.

Now that's funny.

A video blasts behind him.

Babies laughing.

He turns to watch it.

It plays, and he laughs too.

The video eventually rolls over into the thump thump thump of dance music.

He decides to dance.

The lights begin to fade on him.

He is, for the moment, joyous. Oblivious to anything, and everything, that is to come.

The end.

Acknowledgements

My boundless thanks to those folks who helped us with the development of this piece: Jillian Keiley; Danielle Irvine; Leah Lewis; Charlie Browne; David and Karen Hood; Brian Quirt, Jenna Rodgers, and the Banff Playwrights Lab; Aiden Flynn, Krista Hansen, and the staff of the Corner Brook Arts and Culture Centre; Emma Tibaldo and Playwrights' Workshop Montréal; and everyone at the St. John's Short Play Festival.

Robert Chafe is a writer, educator, actor, and arts administrator based in St. John's, Ktaqmkuk (Newfoundland). He has worked in theatre, dance, opera, radio, fiction, and film. His stage plays have been seen in Canada, the United Kingdom, Australia, and in the United States, and include *Oil and Water, Tempting Providence, Afterimage, Under Wraps, Between Breaths*, and *The Colony of Unrequited Dreams* (adapted from the novel by Wayne Johnston). He has been shortlisted twice for the Governor General's Literary Award for Drama and he won the award for *Afterimage* in 2010. He has been a guest instructor at Memorial University, Sir Wilfred Grenfell College, and the National Theatre School of Canada. In 2018 he was awarded an honorary doctorate from Memorial University. He is the playwright and artistic director of Artistic Fraud.

First edition: June 2022
Printed and bound in Canada by Rapido Books, Montreal

Jacket art by Will Gill
Author photo © Ritche Perez

PLAYWRIGHTS
CANADA PRESS

202-269 Richmond St. W.
Toronto, ON
M5V 1X1

416.703.0013
info@playwrightscanada.com
www.playwrightscanada.com
@playcanpress